DEEP INSIDE

by

MIKE WILLMOTT

The Dana, Shrewsbury April - July 2005

Stafford Jail August 2005 - March 2006

Order this book online at www.trafford.com
or email orders@trafford.com

Most Trafford titles are also available at major online book retailers.

Print information available on the last page.

ISBN: 978-1-4251-0989-9 (sc)

Trafford rev. 03/06/2019

Trafford
PUBLISHING® www.trafford.com
North America & international
toll-free: 1 888 232 4444 (USA & Canada)
fax: 812 355 4082

DEDICATION

To all those who helped make my prison stay livable; to my family and friends, for sticking by me, in spite of me, visiting from afar; and to all the people who wrote to me, collectively, a letter a day, for nearly a year; and especially to the Chaplaincies in **HMP THE DANA** and at **HMP STAFFORD**, with particular gratitude to Carol Richardson and the Quaker couple at the latter (Dennis+Joan Gripton) - saints on earth; to the helpful people in Education, the Gym and in Cookery; to Rose Simpson for encouraging me to send off competition entries left, right and centre; to Dorothy Salmon and the *Koestler Trust* for evaluating my work; to *Axis, (Liz and George)* who searched out the root of my problems, and helped heal; to fellow prisoners, who made the place more companionable; to my Probation Officer and *Impact* Counsellor, and *Business Link* and the *Job Centre*, Market Drayton, (David Millington) for helping to re-launch me; to my generous hosts, (the Bateses) who provided a safe haven, and much more, on Home Detention Curfew; finally, to one special correspondent,
who kept my pecker up with a regular supply of challenging cartoons and creative thoughts on life, helping to keep alive 'the unconquerable mind'. (p.48)

INDEX

DEEP INSIDE
A
PRISONER'S RESPONSE
11 MONTHS INSIDE

Arriving in jail as a first timer is shocking, particularly as a 56-year-old, normally 'good' citizen, or 'burgher of this borough'. (Shrewsbury, Shropshire, UK). That's what happened to me on April 7th, 2005, after I had been distressed enough to set fire to my own office at home. Within less than 24 hours of the incident, I was bundled into *The Dana* at Shrewsbury. I had handed myself over to the police because I knew I had done something wrong. I also knew I was ill and needed help. I was at wit's end. Only my public school education prepared me for what was to come.

After librium had helped me down from excess alcohol - over the years (a major contributory factor in the causation of the sorry event) - I set about surviving, on the only terms available. These were my own. Writing was the means by which I tried to make order out of Chaos, or what I later determined was **KAFKA** = the institutional insanity of the prison unsystem. (For my word 'unsystem' Bill Gates has found— 'subsystem; unsystematic; insisted; unassisted; subsystems'. All of these apply horrifically, but I insist, unassisted, on my word—prison was, and is, an *unsystem*. I wrote irregularly but constantly, jotting down everything and anything of interest - to keep the mind alive in this most mind-destroying of places. The Alpha-Omega was my special vehicle - a concise way of getting mind over matter. I stole unashamedly from the books to hand, and then made my A-Z sense of the meat of them. I am eternally grateful for the Quaker book I borrowed from Wednesday's prayer night, the Book of African and West Indian Proverbs, the Deeper Meaning of Life, Bob Harding's poetry, Paul Theroux, The Bible and The Book of Common Prayer. My first saving grace was the Gideon Bible given me on entry. Then the gospel of St Mark I won as a result of a simple competition which set me off on competitions for the Performance Poetry Society, the Koestler Prize, Bridging the Gap and Ottakar's Poetry Prize. Rose Simpson visited valiantly at HMP Stafford to offer encouragement. There was a wonderful hour of performance just after Christmas when prisoners shared talents. That's what I'm doing now, I hope. For any '*outside*' or '*inside*' prisoners. The mind is its own place, and in itself/Can make a heaven of hell, a hell of heaven.' Writing helps self-analysis, making sense, keeping self together - hope. 'Don't let the bastards get you down.' Words rise.

51 MEN IN A CAGE - HMP THE DANA

Warm summer sunshine, peace in the Cage,
apart from the early match-cheering from the Gay Meadow.
51 cons take their afternoon exercise:
a clockwise perambulation round the 100-metre circuit.
One screw stands languidly watching each side:
no action likely – an hour's tedium for them,
outside the tall fence – no contact, lonesome –
imprisoned in their head – time to contemplate
their mental imprisonment: their lives, their wives.
Overhead, the fishing-net strung over the octagon fence
to prevent incoming projectiles, hurled from outside,
over the wall from Castlefields –
half-tennis-balls, loaded with crack.

But shame is not the whole story.
Even encaged, there are common decencies,
common courtesies, and hail-well-mets,
well-wishing for next court appearance,
gentle askings after health, partners, kids;
laughter and stories, experiences and tales:
in the Cage the raconteur thrives.
Also, there's the hum of learning,
where random expertise is shared in short-hand:
drugs, crime, alcohol, punishment, the Outside –
the inevitable, infiltrated with the unusual, or the deep.
The Cage encourages souls to express themselves,
and hidden learnings to be exposed:
Immigration; What happened to the Gold Coast?
Funerals in Ghana; Charles Bronson and the Governor;
Zimbabweans in Hamburg, spreckening Deutsch;
Organic farming; Gangland Telford; Nutrition.

It's not really a cage –
it's not a den of iniquity.
It's a Pandora's box,
producing something rich,
and strange.

HMP COTTAGE INDUSTRIES

SYB

Prisoners make all sorts of things
for other prisoners, in other prisons.
Sudbury, Derbyshire, produces some fine quality foot-wear,
that looks quite classy.
Featherstone, Wolverhampton creates bodywarmers
with jazzy buttons.
All your plastics – combs, toothbrushes, bowls, etc
come from Gartree, Liverpool;
towels and bedding from Wandsworth.

Unfortunately, HMP Full Sutton,
who produce track-suit tops for Shrewsbury
got tangled up with 'Shrewsbury' and 'Shrowsbury',
and managed to shorten it down to **SYB.**
Hundreds of track-suits are wrongly labelled.
Or are they?

Shrewsbury Yob Brigade
Shrewsbury Young Bastards
Shrewsbury Yelling Buggers
Shrewsbury Yawning Bed-pressers
Shrewsbury Yellow Boys
Shrewsbury Yacking Badmouthers
Shrewsbury Yesmen Beanheads
Shrewsbury Yoked-up Bedfellows
Shrewsbury Yuppie Burglars

(or even quite plausibly)

Shrewsbury Youth Band

All is explained – later –
(which it always is – inside - never sooner).
Shrewsbury – SY - Category B (Remand) Prison
becomes, legitimately:

SYB

What a name tag!

ON THE BRIGHTER INSIDE - DOWN THE PAN

Sanitation in the cell has improved since Dickens' day.
Nevertheless, it's a bit rudimentary
to have to sit behind a 3 foot 6 'guard',
staring your cell-mate in the face,
emitting at least unsavoury noises,
and, unfortunately, some cell-filling odours.

But on Day Four in the Dana,
the wretched pan sprang a leak.
We had to have the 'experts' in:
cons earning pocket money.
The one in the blue was passing sixty,
with thick-rimmed glasses.
His 'apprentice' was forty,
though treated like fourteen.

Amidst several 'fuckings',
and lots of spilt water,
it was discovered that the replacement was the wrong size,
and the joint was fitted with a punctured gasket.
(The two Ronnies would have made a better job of it,
though their dialogue wouldn't have been as colourful.)

Mission completed,
after a brief three-quarters-of-an-hour.
At one moment, at least four cons leant over the pan,
observing a screw being twisted in –
(quite fitting, for a prison, with failing outlets).
What professionalism! What finesse! –
Should have been a piece of piss!

Now – testing time, and possibly Eureka.
There was the new pan,
but the last twist of the ear-splitting drill
split the shiny bowl – possibly made in Stoke -
(like most of the druggies in the Dana).

'CUNT!' said the foreman in blue, with his dulled glasses.
We all laughed – like a drain!

3

A THANKSGIVING TO GOD FOR HIS HOUSE

Lord, Thou hast given me a cell
    Wherein to dwell:
A little house, whose humble roof
    Is weather-proof;
Under the spars of which I lie
    Both soft, and dry.
Low is my porch, as is my fate –
    Both void of state;
And yet the threshold of my door
    Is worn by the poor
Who thither come, and freely get
    Good words, or meat.
Like as my parlour, so my hall
    And kitchen's small.
Some brittle sticks of thorn or briar
    Make me a fire,
Close by whose living coal I sit
    And glow like it.
Lord, I confess too, when I dine
    The pule is thine,
And all those other bits, that be
    There placed by Thee –
The worts, the pursloin, and the mess
    Of water-cress.
Thou mak'st my teeming hen to lay
    Her egg each day.
All these, and better Thou dost send
    Me to this end
That I should render, for my part,
    A thankful heart.

A THANKSGIVING TO TO GOD FOR HIS CELL

Lord, Thou hast given me a cell
    Wherein to dwell:
A little house, whose humble roof
    Is weather-proof;
Under the frame of which I lie
    Both high and dry.
Strait is my gate, as is my fate,
    Both void of mate.
And yet the threshold of my door
    Brings friends out with Law,
Who thither come, and freely get
    Good words, and chat.
My 'parlour' is my only stall -
    Little space at all:
Some simple things – a bed, a chair
    Fulfil desire:
A table plain by which I sit
    And write on it.
Lord, I confess too, when I dine
    The fare is fine.
And all the things that come to me
    Were meant to be:
The letters, the thoughts, the mess
    That is my case.
I strive each thread to neatly lay
    Resolved each day
Determined for my best self to fend
    For better end,
That I with cleaner, stiller heart,
    May soon depart.

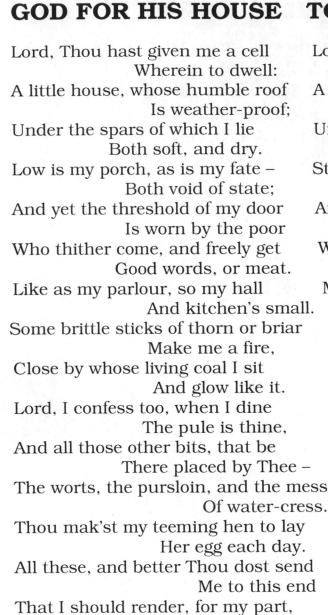

Robert Herrick 1591-1674

Michael Willmott HMP Stafford 2005-6

A REDUCED AUTHORIZED VERSION (ST. JAMES) OF THE NATIVITY OF JESUS CHRIST

IN 90 WORDS

(A competition for *The Church of England Newspaper*)

A. ANNUNCIATION – ANGEL GABRIEL TO MARY (Lk.1 26-56)
B. BIRTH - "ON THIS WISE." @ BETHLEHEM (Mt. 1. 18)
C. CENSUS -_+ ROMAN TAXATION (Lk. 2 1-5)
D. DAVID – CITY + LINEAGE (Lk.2 1-5)
E. EMMANUEL = "GOD WITH US" (Mt. 1.23)
F. FATHER – JOSEPH (Mt. 1.20)
G. GOD – THE FATHER (Jn. 1.1)
H. HEAVEN vs HEROD (Mt. 2. 16)
I. INNKEEPER – "NO ROOM" (Lk.2.7)
J. JOHN – (Mk 1 1-18)
K. KNOWLEDGE – (CARNAL) – MARY – NONE (Lk 1-27)
L. LIGHT – (Jn. 1.1)
M. MANGER –(Lk. 2 7)
N. NAZARETH – JOSEPH'S HOMETOWN (Lk.2. 1-4)
O. "OUT OF EGYPT" – ESCAPE (Mt.2 13-15)
P. PROPHECY – ISAIAH – "BEHOLD A VIRGIN" (Isaiah 7. 14)
Q. Q.A.JOHN THE BAPTIST:
   "I AM NOT THE CHRIST." (Jn 1.20)
R. RAMA – VOX IN RAMA – THE INNOCENTS (Mt.2.18)
S. SHEPHERDS – "SORE AFRAID" (Lk. 2.9)
T. TREASURES – GOLD, FRANKINCENSE, MYRRH (Mt. 2.11)
U. UNCTION – "YE HAVE AN UNCTION" (1Jn.2.20)
V. VIRGIN ANNA – GAVE THANKS (Lk.2.37)
W. WAY – "PREPARE YE THE WAY" (Is.7.14)
X. XRISTOS – (GREEK WORD FOR CHRIST)
Y. YEARS – 46 YEARS TEMPLE – 3 DAYS (RESURRECTION)
   (Jn.2.20)
Z. ZACHARIA'S ELIZABETH CONCEIVED (Lk 40-48)

AMEN!

HALLELUJAH!

PAX VOBISCUM!

5

A FESTIVAL OF NINE (STAFFORD) CAROLS 2005

O come, O come Emmanuel

O come, O come, Emmanuel,
The truth to us the hopeful, faithful, tell,
That mourn in lonely exile here,
But wait in constant prayer, without fear.
Rejoice! Rejoice! Emmanuel
Shall come right here, in this humble chapel.

Once in royal David's city

Once in royal David's city,
Jesus came, our souls to cheer.
Not in a poor lowly stable
Will we see Him, but right here.
Jesus wants to meet us now,
Let our heads before Him bow.

It came upon the midnight clear

It came upon the midnight clear,
Two thousand years ago,
Our destined Saviour brought us cheer –
We cannot say Him –'No.'
"Peace on the earth, good will to men,"
The angels sang on high.
Like shepherds we down here below
Should greet Him coming nigh.

Lo He comes, with clouds descending

Lo, He comes, with clouds descending,
Once for favoured sinners slain,
Now for prisoners interceding,
Helping make their future plain.
Hallelujah! Hallelujah! Hallelujah!
God appears for those enchained.

Silent night
Silent night, holy night,
Sleeps the world, hid from sight.
Pray for poor sinners who lie like us –
Inside – or outside – no need to discuss –
Praying for heavenly rest,
Praying for heavenly rest.

In the bleak mid-winter
In the bleak mid-winter,
Many wait alone;
Weather cold, unfriendly,
Or reasons else to moan.
"Love came down at Christmas,"
The carollers express.
In the bleak mid-winter
Let's take Him for our own.

Unto us a boy is born

Unto us a boy is born,
King of liberation.
Not a time for us to mourn:
Let's sing in adoration.

Hark the herald angels sing

Hark the herald angels sing,
Glory to our new-born King.
Peace on earth and mercy mild,
God and sinners reconciled.
Joyful all ye nations rise.
Join the triumph of the skies.
With the angelic hosts proclaim,
Christ is born in Bethlehem.
Hark, the herald angels sing,
Glory to the new-born King.

Hark, for fellow Christians sing,
Glory to our new-born King.
Peace to us, and mercy mild,
Us and victims reconciled.

Joyful all us prisoners rise,
Join Christ's triumph over lies.
With our loved ones on our side,
Worship Christ by all allied.
Hark, our fellow Christians sing
Glory to our new-born King.

O come, all ye faithful

O come all us faithful,
Inmates in this prison.
O come we, O come we to our fine chapel.
Come and respect Him,
Born to be our Saviour.
O come let us adore Him,
O come let us respect Him,
O come let us pronounce Him,
Christ for Stafford!

Born for us sinners,
Light for our redemption.
O speed us towards our closer, clean release.
Come and adore Him,
Born the King of angels.
O come let us adore Him,
O come let us respect Him,
O come let us pronounce Him
Christ for Stafford.

Sing choirs of convicts,
Sing in expectation,
O sing every person in this whole community.
Come and respect Him
Born to be our Saviour.
O come let us adore Him,
O come let us respect Him,
O come let us pronounce Him Christ for Stafford.

FR XMAS' txt msg

where r u? mrsx
lost. frx
where lost? mrsx
fi nu I wunt b lost. frx
nt funny. Diner n'ly redi. mrsx
rudolph nose went out in fog. lost. frx
told u it was goin dim!!! still fogi? mrsx
no – fog gone bt dunt recognise were am now. frx
describe. mrsx
big pointy stone things and camels. frx
u in egypt. mrsx
2morrow i sack rudolph. frx
i give dinner to elves. mrsx
i is sorry. frx
not haf as sorry is u will be !!! mrsx

with thanks to Mike Harding for cheering up Christmas

AN ALPHA-OMEGA OF THE UP-SIDE OF INSIDE

A. The absence of Outside pressures - **ABSENCE**
   phonecalls, job worries, tax, VAT – other people's
   expectations.
B. Free banking, with controlled supply of **BANKING**
   survival cash, and unseen savings Outside.
C. Cooked Saturday and Sunday **COOKED BREAKFAST**
   breakfast, or at least half of it – porridge, fry-up (no proper
   coffee).
D. From Roast Beef and Yorkshire **DIET**
   Pudding to Jamaican Beef Rojan, rice and peas – various
   nourishment. Always 350 calories a meal minimum + fruit.
E. Time to re-arrange and re-discover **EDUCATION**
   what you know, and trip over fascinating new stuff, with
   time to spare.

F. Companions, comforters, inspirers, **FELLOW PRISONERS**
communicators, eye-openers – stability.

G. Gym, with £25,000 equipment for **GYM**
body-building, time-passing, fat-destroying, muscle-toning,
relaxing, activity.

H. A seemingly unending supply of hot water, **HOT WATER**
to clean dishes, and bodies, freely – HYGIENE.

I. From a correspondent, an article, a piece **INSPIRATION**
a remembered comment, a hopeful act.

J. Like the one about the hamster and the gold-fish: **JOKES**
What's the difference between a hamster and a goldfish, (in
prison terms)? The hamster gets out of the cage fit; the
gold-fish just goes 'glug'.

K. Kitchen-cleaning done by a team of paid **KITCHEN**
inmates away from hassle-free 'residents': no pots and pans –
meals regular and punctual.

L. Free regular laundry, done by someone else: **LAUNDRY**
no ironing, no soap-suds, no unsightly, threatening piles: job
done!

M. On site Pharmacy, with free pain-killers, **MEDICINE**
instant supplies of specialist tablets on request – Health
Farm – Rehab.

N. A small but same-day supply, with time **NEWSPAPERS**
to read every necessary word, absorb and be up-to-date.

O. A rare but wonderful experience, when **OFFICIAL HELP**
an officer improves conditions, encourages, enables.

P. Inconquerable power to see beyond the present, **PRAYER**
to absorb the past, to prepare for the future: to re-pair.

Q. Anything – even *'The Weakest Link'* – that keeps **QUIZES**
the brain working – cross-words, Sudoku,etc.

R. Total re-start, having stripped self **RECONSTRUCTION**
down and put on your new body, mind, soul, potential –
future!

S. Snatched from an organist, a nurse, **SMILES**
a photo, a visitor, a cell-mate, a tv actor – anywhere positive.

T. Used wisely, a means of catching up with past best **T.V.**
of British, present news, classic – whole – films – interest –
LIFE.

U. A conversation, a letter, an article, **UNEXPECTED**
a documentary, a passing remark: something un-grey.

V. A reminder of normality, sanity, trust, love, faith **VISITS** in your future: light through the tunnel.

W. Regular infusion of ecumenical Christianity; *'The* **WORSHIP** *Heaven and Earth Show'*, and *'Songs of Praise'* raising the spirit. Monday bible video, HMP The Dana; Wednesday Prayer Meeting, HMP Stafford.

X. Rare – but the flutter at the approach of **XCITEMENT** 'Canteen', with the Friday night *Hamlet* cigar. *(weekly groceries)*

Y. All the civilised answers, the fulfilment of **YES** requests, the polite smiles on the Route – the prison flowers and plants, particularly the lavender for cell-aroma, and the Xmas point-settias from the VP green-house.*(vulnerable person)*

Z. Some of the wilder inmates, with mop-head **ZANINESS** dreadlocks, pipe-cleaning sticks and ecstatic voices.

AN OMEGA-ALPHA
OF THE DOWN-SIDE OF INSIDE

Z. Wild men of Africa and the Caribbean whose **ZULUS** voices reach unbearable levels during battles of chequers.

Y. Yells from 'The Block' after midnight, when **YELLS** the live shriek from Hell.

X. Fellow prisoners assured they know how to **XPERTS** do everything – judge your case, do your job, live your life.

W. Waste of time, waste of people-power, waste of **WASTE** resources, litter, waste of food: above all, waste of spirit.

V. Restriction to nineteenth-century brick vistas – no **VIEWS** horizons, countryside, trees, humans, roads away from Stafford.

U. The absence of reasonable answers to **UNREASON** reasonable questions, like "Why are we waiting?"

T. When you are not consuming time, but time-watching, **TIME** time not slipping by – queues, delays, postponements.

S. The worst example of macho male behaviour- **SPITTING** worse than swearing – worse than nude cell wall-paper.

R. The only means by which information, and **RUMOUR** mis-information, is conveyed along the corridors of unempowerment.

Q. Searching for reasonableness, **QUESTIONS UNANSWERED** for explanations about rules, bureaucracy – zero intelligence.

P. Obscure rules e.g. about stamped addressed **PETTINESS** envelopes being held in Reception : LSD; £sd; fraud?

O. The inevitable assertion of an unreal, **ONE-UP-MAN-SHIP** undeserved pecking order on the level plain of prison.

N. Or absence of the real thing, except by interminable **NEWS** repeats on telly: absence of good news from nowhere.

M. A sadistic advance upon masochism, in which **MACHOCHISM** 'hards' inflict their bullying tactics: officers and men, (and women) in the gym, in the cells, with untamed ghetto-blasters, sagging fags, with the klaxon and the indecipherable shouting from landing to landing: cacophony.

K. Institutionalised, unorganised, organisational **KAFKA** insanity: 'Applications' in bottles washed out to the sea of inefficiency.

J. People sending Christmas cards in **JOB'S COMFORTERS** July, or referring tactlessly to unattainable normalities (eg e-mail).

I. The excessive navel-gazing that happens **INTROSPECTION** particularly at long periods of Bang-Up 5pm-8.30am w-ends.

H. The assumption that VPs **HYPOCRISY** ('Vulnerable People' + sex offenders) are in a different level of criminality, permitting vile, unproven condemnation.

G. The apparent toughness of the bully, too **GUTLESSNESS** cowardly to recognise his own weakness.

F. An inability to see – or to be allowed to **FUTURELESSNESS** see a way ahead: blank, systematic, despair: infectious.

E. The most wild accounts of criminal success, **EXAGGERATION** power, 'privilege' on the outside: lies, damned lies!

D. About yourself, your conduct, your **DISAPPOINTMENTS** relationships, your past, your present, your future: you.

C. By word of mouth – deep-throated **COMMUNICATIONS** shouts as in Billingsgate Fish Market, designed to blur meaning.

B. Not simply doing nothing, or nothing meaningful: **BOREDOM** Workshop Five (and probably 1-10).

A. Absence of freedom, sanity, loved ones, loved **ABSENCE** things communication, beauty, fun, colour – LIFE.

JAIL-HOUSE ROCK OR MUSIC BEHIND BARS

A grey afternoon in January;
Christmas in the bin;
the future at best nondescript –
mostly bleak – with no prospect of daffodils.

8 amorphous gents, mostly black –
if not in skin, in heart, or supposed to be –
cons – at the seat of musical learning,
in a grey industrial room, in grey mode.

Equipment exists – 8 functional Yamahas
(for 8 bottom-of-the-line, off the line, 'students',)
four garish guitars, all red and plastic –
and 1 advanced computer, with 'Cu-base', apparently.

Already mayhem rules, with all systems on
at maximum decibels: head-phones paralytically helpless.
The carefree, blond-locked teacher expounds the basics –
"Just a bit of theory, some 12-bar blues, 6 weeks – you're away."

The art of music is reduced to five basic chords –
"All you need for the complete works of Beatles/Oasis."
"Count your beats – can be 3 or 4."
"Know your scales and keys."
No room for grey areas.

Cacophony rules – hints of Bach Partitas,
James Blunt, calypso, Garage Music;
rhythms of the pounding of musclemen in the gym,
sound-waves apart from music:
Blake's Hell.

But out of it comes enlightenment, in unexpected doses:
the fingering for the scale of F major in three octaves;
the intricacies of the pentatonic scale;
the flattened sixth, and G minor 7's:
harmony's mystery.

Above all, the wonder of chords and progressions,
The modulations of Taizé's harmonies, and Satie's magic:
Simplicities in sounds and sequences;
Music's filigreed net cast over the languishing soul.

Rescue – until, without warning, they cancelled it.
No reasons given, beyond numbers, exam entries,
'Basic Skills', finance cut-backs.
Music - a basic human right - violated: RAPE!

MACHOCHISM

Like its sister vice, masochism,
machochism involves wilful pain, inflicted on others,
for pleasure, in a confined space.
Prison is the ultimate confined space.
It is an anthill of iniquity – the Accra of the uncivilised world,
from Stafford, to Auschwitz, to Guantanemo Bay.
'Machochism' is my neologism –
an ugly term, for an ugly activity –
something that happens spontaneously,
bursting naturally unnaturally between people,
like a fat zit exploding.
It can be ferocious, large, public –
like the queer gang-bang at the climax of '*SCUM*',   *(borstal film)*
when the three cons ram the holy innocent in the green-house,
with the queer screw in blind surveillance.
It can be short, outwardly quiet, but shocking,
like the gormless screw exerting his thick, pompous power
by saying 'No', to a reasonable request,
by a timid, blank-eyed con
wanting to deliver his match-sticked present
to his partner on Visit.
At worst, it is not brave enough to be face to face,
but comes under the door of the cell -
unannounced - from the 7 Governors –
unwise, unknown, unseen givers of the *D Cat* –   *(Open Prison Status)*
confirmation of last week's decision rescinded unexplained
for the wide-eyed Jamaican
who'd promised his daughter he'd see her for Christmas.
Most threatening, is the in-cell unbridled bully,
who sizes up to you, body to body, nose to nose,
and shouts the most vituperative, black abuse at you –
"Mother-fucking, white shit-scum!
Why you take no SHOWA?"
There's no recourse to reason, authority, right –
just pained reception of the unbridled hatefulness:
nasty, brutish, short – breeding only one good thing –
resolution never to ever let absolute power
corrupt you absolutely.

ARSON

Ugly word, arson.
Ugly, thing – wild pyromania;
demonic destructiveness;
mindless defiance;
fires of hatred – intolerance.

Was it Guy Fawkes the guy,
or the Pope,
or all the popery
they burnt to cinders?
Or was it their own hatred -
Milton's 'self-consuming fire'?

Now French incendiary fires -
fires of desperation last autumn,   (2005)
lit by the unenfranchised.

Wild – like that mad thing
of setting fire to old leaves
mocked by Bob Newhart
phoning Nutty Sir Wal Raleigh
after he'd discovered spuds –
"You roll up these leaves in a tube....
And then you set fire to it, hunh?"

Arson in Law
is right up against Murder.
Ignition is guilt, trial, sentence, imprisonment,
melted down into one –
no half-way houses:
just burnt-out ones.
There's little crawling out of the wreckage.
"Five years – didn't you do well?"
'Mindless act of violence'
is assumed mindless,
and the mind's prevented from speaking
to defend itself. Indefensible.
The voice that is crying out for attention
is smothered for attention-seeking.
A criminal danger to society.

No need for fair trial.
A fire-blanket thrown by the legal attendants:
'Send him down.'
To the fires of hell.
His lonely fires.

But autumnal fires have the power of purging,
purifying the bugged soil for spring planting.
And the light of the fire,
and the excitement,
the cleansing of fire
can heal encrustations.

Hot pokers make punch.
'The evening comes
with smell of steaks in passage-ways..
the burnt-out ends of smoky days.'
Fire can redeem –
not just insurance policies –
but whole souls.

The phoenix rises out of the ashes,
flutters his wings,
shakes the dust off his feathers,
and off his shoes,
and walks free.
Flies free.
Fired up.
On fire.

AN ALPHA-OMEGA OF WEST INDIAN PROVERBS

A. Ole (old) fiddle play new tune.   **ABILITY**
    (Jamaican)

B. Beauty widout(without)grace like rose widout smell. **BEAUTY**
    (Jamaican)

C. Hen da cackle an 'joyment himself, him no   **CARELESSNESS**
    know say hawk da watch him.   (Jamaican)
    (The hen that cackles and enjoys himself
    doesn't see the hawk that watches him.)

D. If you get you han' in a debil mout', tek time tek   **DANGER**
    i' out.   (Jamaican)
    If you get your hand inside the devil's mouth,
    take time in removing it.

E. Bald head soon shabe. (shaved)   **EASE**
    (Jamaican)

F. It's the knife that knows the heart of the yam. **FAMILIARITY**
    (Haitian)

G. Pack ob (of) cards de debil's (devil's) prayer-book. **GAMBLING**
    (Jamaican)

H. 'Too-much-hurry' get dey to-morra, 'tek-time' get dey **HASTE**
today.

'Too-much-hurry' gets there tomorrow; 'take-time' gets there today.

I. Follow fashion bruk (broke) monkey neck. **IMITATION**

J. Happiness is the greatest doctor in the world. **JOY**

(Haitian)

K. If you follow wha' riber carry, you neber drink **KNOWLEDGE**
de water. (Jamaican)

If you consider what the river carries, you'll never drink the water.

L. Dem short fe singer when dem put peacock a choir. **LACK**
They're short of a singer when they put the peacock in the choir.

(Jamaican)

M. Spiteful man put peppah da he mout' **MALICE**
fo' blow dutty out a-he matty yeye. (Guyanan)

The spiteful man puts pepper in his mout to blow dirt out of his friend's eye.

N. If you nyam egg, you mus' bruk de shell. **NECESSITY**
If you eat an egg, you must break the shell. (Jamaican)

O. De more yuh (you) watch, de less yuk see. **OBSERVATION**
('Bajan' = Barbadian)

P. Wha' (t) de (the) goat do, de kid follow.(Jamaican) **PARENTS**

Q. Bad t (h)ing no hab (have) owner. (Jamaican) **QUALITY**

R. When two big bottle deh (there) a-table (on the table) **RANK**
little wan (one) no bu (s) iness. (Guyanan)

S. 'Tak kyar,' de mudda ob safety. ('Take care' is the **SAFETY**
mother of safety.) (Jamaican)

T. Nothing dries faster than tears. **TEARS**

U. The fish on the grill is not afraid of burning. **UNCONCERN**

V. Good sometin' easy fe fling 'way, but hard **VALUE**
to pick up. (Jamaican)

W. De (the) soldier's blood, de general's name.(Jamaica) **WAR**

X. A hass (horse's) good heart mek (makes) **(E)XPLOITATION**
man a-ride (him) as he like. (Guyanan)

Y. You see eberybody (everybody) run, tek (take) **YOU**
time. (Jamaican)

Z. Who no know dead, lek ' look 'pon sleep. **ZZ**
Who doesn't know death, let him look upon sleep. (Jamaican)

A RIPOSTE TO THOMAS HARDY

*on learning about sickle cells, haemoglobin,
malaria and healing powers – even for cancer, alcoholism, etc*

HEREDITY – THOMAS HARDY
I am the family face.
Flesh perishes, I live on,
Projecting trait and trace
Through time to time anon,
And leaping from place to place
Over oblivion.
The years-heired feature then can
In curve and voice and eye
Despise the human span
Of durance – that is I;
The eternal thing in man,
That heeds no call to die.

GENE – MICHAEL WILLMOTT
I am the family gene.
Flesh perishes, I live on.
Now Science lets me be seen
In not unchangeable bond.
While chromosomes still teem
Dull desperation would be fond.
The years-heired feature now can
In bone and cell and vein
Be transformed in the human span
And break the inevitable chain.
Hardy can die - a spam -
Hope can live again.

19

THE LEGAL SYSTEM

The first thing is
it's not a system, truly.
It's systematically unsystematic.

A system is something designed for a purpose.
The legal 'system' starts off rudderless
in a mass of self-inflicted complication,
heading nowhere.

Reverentially, it's headed by the Judiciary.
That's the long-arm, pseudo-intellectual Arm of the Law,
continuing and complicating the injudicious acts of the fuzz.

Like the world of Kafka, it thrives on being unknown,
unknowable, unapproachable, indecipherable,
unanswerable, inscrutable, unapologetic.
Like *Jarndyce and Jarndyce,*
"It just grinds on, slow and thin",
handing out life-long sentences, in inexorable paragraphs.

Instead of desperate invoking of 'Recourse to Justice',
the unsuspecting fly should never approach the sticky web.
Fine advice, impossibly *post hoc.*
Like the Irishman's advice to the lost traveller –
"Well, if I were you,
I wouldn't have started from here at all, at all."
The knowing advice is, "Don't start off at all,
in the direction of the 'system'."

The exigencies of Legality are imprisonment's best deterrent.
It is a quiet Leviathan, a twisted Behemoth.
Like Blair's God, next time, best defence is,
"We don't do it."

AN ALPHA-OMEGA UPON THE PSALMS

A. Psalm 54 vs1 "Save me, O God for thy Name's sake: **AVENGE** and avenge me in thy strength."

B. Psalm 118 vs 26 "Blessed be he that cometh in the **BLESSED** name of the Lord: we have wished you good luck, ye that are of the house of the Lord."

C. Psalm 142 vs 1 "I cried unto the Lord with my voice: **CRY** yea, even unto the Lord did I make my supplication."

D. Psalm 107 vs 9-10 "For he satisfieth the empty soul: **DEATH** and filleth the hungry soul with goodness. Such as sit in darkness, and in the shadow of death: being fast bound in misery and iron."

E. Psalm 39 vs 5 "Lord, let me know mine end, and the **END** number of my days: that I may be certified how long I have to live."

F. Psalm 39 vs 5 "The fear of the Lord is the beginning of **FEAR** wisdom: a good understanding have all they that do thereafter."

G. Psalm 19 vs 1 "The heavens shall declare the glory of **GOD** God: and the firmament showeth his handy-work."

H. Psalm 118 vs 22 "The same stone which the **HEADSTONE** builder refused: is become the headstone in the corner."

I. Psalm 119 vs 113 "I hate them that imagine evil **I** things: but thy law do I love."

J. Psalm 122 vs 3;6 "Jerusalem is built as a **JERUSALEM** city: that is at unity in itself. O pray for the peace of Jerusalem: they shall prosper that love thee."

K. Psalm 24 vs 7 "Lift up your heads, O ye gates: and be ye**KING** lift up, ye everlasting doors: and the King of Glory shall come in."

L. Psalm 37 vs 32 "The law of his God is in his heart: and his goings shall not slide."

M. Psalms 67 vs 1 "God be merciful unto us, and bless **MERCY** us: and shew the light of his countenance upon us."

N. Psalm 115 vs 1 "Not unto us, O Lord, not unto us, **NOT** but unto thy Name give the praise, for thy loving mercy and for thy truth's sake."

O. Psalm 71 16 "Forsake me not, O God, in mine **OLD AGE** old age, when I am old and grey-headed: until I have showed thy strength unto this generation, and thy power to all them."

P. Psalm 135 1 "O praise the Lord, laud ye the name of **PRAISE** the Lord: praise it, O ye servants of the Lord."

Q. Psalm 127 vs 5-6 "Happy is the man that hath **QUIVERFUL** his quiver full of them. Like as the arrows in the hand of the giant."

R. Psalm 90 vs 1 "Lord, thou hast been our refuge: **REFUGE** from one generation to another."

S. Psalm 113 vs 6 "He taketh up the simple out of the **SIMPLE** dust: and lifteth the poor out of the mire."

T. Psalm 146 vs 2 "O put not your trust in princes, nor **TRUST** in any child of man: for there is no help in them."

U. Psalm 119 vs 103-4 "O how sweet are thy **UNDERSTANDING** words unto my throat: yea, sweeter than honey unto my mouth."

V. Psalm 94 vs 1 "O Lord God, to whom vengeance **VENGEANCE** belongeth : O God to whom vengeance belongeth, shew thyself."

W. Psalm 128 vs 3 "Thy wife shall be as the fruitful vine: **WIFE** upon the walls of thy house. Thy children like the olive branches: round about thy table."

X. Psalm 8 vs 1 "O Lord our Governor, how **(E)XCELLENT** excellent is Thy name in all the world."

Y. Psalm 90 vs 1 "For a thousand years in Thy sight **YEARS** are but as yesterday: seeing that is past as a watch in the night."

Z. Psalm 125 vs 1 "They that put their trust in the Lord **ZION** shall be even as the mount Zion: which may not be removed, but lasts for ever."

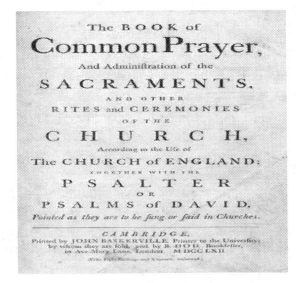

SERVING TEA-TIME

Formerly enjoying coffee-addiction,
and others even more damaging –
tea took over on Day One.
The freebie sachets of "dust-bags" set the trend.
Then the mucho-cheapo *Happy Shopper* box
was the closest ally on the cell mini-dining-table.
The kettle was exhausted with overwork,
for ever bubbling to boiling-point,
and swamping the limp, grey sachet,
with steaming brew.
The merits of whether to add milk before or after
became a matter of moot point,
and a prelapserian word, of latinate origin,
sprang back to mind –
(To cell-guests) – "Are you a prelacterian?"
(That would have Wedgwood Benn flummoxed.)

Chagrin set in because the used bags couldn't be composted,
but just dumped dejectedly amongst the rest of the detritus.
There was the thought of saving them for re-use.
But a bounteous, non-stop supply
permitted the luxury of instant ejection –
like casting excess baggage out of the plane
to prevent disaster in aerial turbulence....
Coming to tannin –
if the inside of my stomach's
coloured anything like the inside of my plastic cup,
then it's a pretty sorry, murky sight:
I just hope the effect is decorative rather than malignant.
Tea-time served no purpose,
save for the comfort of the cup,
the sharing of the brew,
the warmness of the liquid,
and the watering of the habit.
One thing it had nothing to do with
was Earl Grey, or even Brook Bond.
Closer in taste and look
to the water used to swab out the cell floor.
What a decline for the British Imperial beverage!

THE RANDOM URINE SAMPLE

OR

TAKING THE PISS

Rude awakening at 8.0 a.m. Monday morning.
Jangle of keys, and the dour officiousness of Mr Haddock,
stern moustachioed, and in business mode.
I was escorted into a surprisingly smart cell –
in fact, a double cell, joined by a hole in the wall,
down in the bowels of *The Dana* on "The Ones".
It was spic and span, and business-like - like Mr Haddock.
He'd muttered something about "Random Urine Sample"
at my cell door, but there was too much interference
from his moustache, and his Black Country lips.

He sat me down – all official – as if we were at Immigration,
though I knew we weren't: this was my Im-mobile Home.
His large colleague –
('Screws' only come in 3 sizes – X-Large, lanky or squat) –
was busily tapping the keys, or swivelling the chair
to enable him to jettison a folder into a suitable tray.

"Now what we're doing is all above board and harmless
 – if you're clear –
and I'm here to tell you about 'procedures'.
It happens every month, on the first day of the month.
Hence, as you'll notice - if you're awake -
it's the first of August, and you've been selected...
Nothing sinister," he added – sinisterly.
"The '*Compulsory*' Urine Sample is for those on drugs,
And on the results depends the prisoner's future."
Instant re-assurance – there's nothing running in my urine,
now that the demon Alcohol has been banished.
"So I'll read you your rights, and keep you informed,
so that you can see we're not taking the piss –
in a manner of speaking," – he added, proud of his joke.
"It's all computerised, so all the random numbers match,
and you can see and check everything I do –
there's no interference, or rigging the evidence –
your urine will speak for itself."

The mind boggled.
It was like being in a cellar in a château in France,
watching the finer processes of vintage production...
except when next door, standing over the urinal
(watched by CCTV – an embarrassing intrusion)
the "vintage production" wouldn't come.
I'm there, holding the plastic cylinder nursingly near my pipe,
Praying for my bladder to be a good boy,
But, oh no! Embarrassment!
Shyness and muscular atrophy.
Nothing would drip.
I felt a total, utter failure.
The cup of prison-pipe water had no immediate effects,
and Mr Haddock warned I'd be rationed to 1 per ½ hour:
"Rules and Regulations – so as to get a true sample."
He helpfully switched on the taps,
but the sound of the water pipes and the running of the water
would not unlock my urinary tract.
I took half an hour off, and read "*Maxim*",
which suggested it's hard in the Gents
when you're standing by your boss,
and natural inhibitions prevent free flow.
I asked Mr Haddock what was the record?
He said ominously, "Five hours."
I remembered my father on bell-ringers' outings
admiring Harry Crabbe's bladder,
which could survive an onslaught of five or six pints
without putting him under pressure till the next stop.

Then it came to me –
it was the pill I'd taken just before 8 am –
Allopurinoll – to fight off the dreaded uric acid,
the gout-making chemical in my ancient bones.
It was to be taken with food, and with masses of cups of water.
The Dana having been built in mid 19th century,
I had been suspicious of the liquid
trickling limply from rusty, dusty pipes.
The water is probably Victorian too,
So I took none with the pill.
Hence, total dehydration.

After mild guffaws and encouragement from Mr H
I made a last attempt at 10 am,
and managed a very fine 2 inches
of solid orange liquid – Kia-Ora worthy,
magnificently reaching the regulation line.
Mr Haddock was chuffed and relieved.
I was relieved, and chuffed.
He could get on with the official wrapping up,
the matching-up of barcodes,
the sealing and labelling.

A piece of piss!

AN ALPHA-OMEGA OF CRIMINAL QUOTATIONS

A. Neville Heath, the Acid Bath Killer, accepting the **ALCOHOL**
hangman's offer of a glass of whisky as he walked to
the scaffold: "You might as well make that a double."

B. Thomas McGuiness, Scottish murderer, offered **BRANDY**
a tot of brandy by the hangman: "I have been a
teetotaller all my days, and I'll manage without it now."

C. Joyce Turner, mother of six, on murdering **CONVENIENCE**
her 'lazy good-for-nothing bum' husband: "He always
wanted to die in bed. I merely arranged it, that's all."

D. Leon Murant, recaptured while reading a **DISAPPOINTMENT**
newspaper report of his escape from a French prison:
"I never had time to get to the end of the article."

E. Donald 'Pee Wee' Gaskins, serial killer, while **EQUAL RIGHTS**
on Death Row awaiting execution: "I never heard of no
women-libbers demanding their equal rights when
it comes to capital punishment."

F. John Haigh dissolved six victims in a drum of **FOOLPROOF**
sulphuric acid. "How can you prove murder if there is no body?"

G. Dr. William Palmer, Victorian mass murderer, **GALLOWS**
on the gallows at Stafford Gaol: "Are you sure this thing is safe?"

H. Charlie Peace, Victorian burglar and murderer, on **HYMNS**
singing hymns: "Makes a man feel nearer 'is Maker, to sing them
lovely tunes."

I. Howard Marks, international drug-dealer, to police**INVENTION**
as they broke down his door in a 2 a.m. raid: " I suppose you've
come about the T.V. licence?"

J. Robert Stroud, The Birdman of Alcatraz, and a **JAILBIRD**
homosexual, as described by a fellow prisoner: "He was
as attractive as a barracuda.'

K. Christa Lehmann, German woman **KOOKS AND CRAZIES**
who killed her husband, her in-laws and a friend: "I don't
suppose I should have done it, but I love to go to funerals."

L. Ned Kelly, Australian bushranger as he stood **LIFE**
on the scaffold at Melbourne in 1880: "Ah well, I suppose it had
to come to this. Such is life."

M. Christopher Craig, convicted with **MISAPPREHENSION**
Bentley of the murder of PC Miles in 1982: "What I've never been
able to understand is how I shot him between the eyes when he
was facing away from me and was going the wrong way."

N. Lifer Bernard Coy, trying to interest **NONCHALANCE**
convict Clarence Carnes in an escape plot: "How much time you
doin'? Life?" Carnes: "No. Ninety years."

O. William Rees-Davies QC's first question **OPENING QUESTION**
to a prosecution witness: "Smith, you're a liar, aren't you?"

P. French serial killer Henry Landru from the dock **POLITENESS**
to female spectators who packed his murder trial: "I wonder if
there is any lady present who would care to take my seat?"

Q. Taravingia Howe, a Zimbabwean asked by a **QUOTA**
magistrate why he stole 757 sweaters, 733 men's shirts, 460
dresses, 403 jackets, 83 pairs of socks + 286 pairs of children's
trousers worth circa £14,000 said: "I have a large family."

R. Reggie Kray, asked on his deathbed why he had **REASONS**
killed McVitie: "Because he was a vexation to the spirit."

S. Mr Justice Laws, picking up on Michael **SCRABBLED**
Mansfield QC's use of the word 'analogise' in an IRA trial: "Is
there such a word?" (Mansfield) "There is, as a matter of fact."
(Justice Laws): "It comes from playing too much Scrabble."

T. Ronnie Kray: "How can you ask me to pay any tax? **TAX**
I'm a madman."

U. Mr Justice Avery, hearing an appeal of **UNDERSTATEMENT**
Major Herbert Armstrong, convicted of poisoning his wife: "To
find a packet of three and a half grains of white arsenic in a
solicitor's pocket is surely rare?"

V. "On the judge's direction, do you find the defendants **VERDICT**
guilty or not guilty of insider dealing?"
Forewoman, after a long pause: "Not sure."

W. Sam Giancana, Mafia Godfather. "Women are like **WOMEN** shoes. Wear them out, throw them away."

X. Margaret Allen, a bus conductress, explaining why **'XCUSE** she had battered to death another woman: "I was in one of my funny moods."

Y. George Smith, shouting at Mr. Justice **YES, MINISTER** Scrutton summing up in the 'Brides in the Bath' trial: "You'll have me hung the way you are going on! Sentence me and have done with it! It's a disgrace to a Christian country, this is!"

Z. Howard Unruh to police who arrested **ZERO INTELLIGENCE** him for shooting dead thirteen people in twelve minutes: "I'm no psycho. I have a good mind. I'm not a murderer, though I may be a bit peculiar!"

AN EPISTLE BY CHILDREN TO GOD

from *Children's Letters to God, 1975*

If you go into a church or a cathedral and there's a board for pinning prayers, inquisitiveness is uncontainable. Outside Princess Diana's house, outside King's Cross Station 7/7, at the spot where Andrew Walker was axed down, were placed some of the most poignant human responses imaginable. I tripped over a 1975 edition of *"Children's Letters to God"* in the prison library. It was American, with American cultural references - which didn't suit my predilections, but the sentiments were international - blow the references. The editors claimed rightly – "All of them are addressed to God with much hope."

There will be at least one that will leap from the page for you with terrible poignancy: I know where my one is. All are marked by clarity, succinctness, freshness and honesty. Some achieve a theological depth aspired to by most preachers and teachers, but never attained with such nonchalance. The original assortment was somewhat random, and a mixed bag of memorability. I have 'heard the whole offering in my head', and shaped it into one corporate, orderly letter to God, with sub-sections. I am obviously indebted to the original editors – Stuart Hample and Eric Marshall. I wish I could reproduce some of the illustrations. Mostly, I am indebted to 'the mouths of babes and sucklings', which were precocious enough to spring these gems upon me. They don't deserve to stay behind bars. (The gems that is.)

Dear God, -

ORIGINS

Where does everybody come from? I hope you can explain it better than my father.

Why did you make so many people? Could you make another earth and put the extras there?

When you made the first man, did he work as good as we do now?

In bible times did they really talk that fancy? Are there any patriarchs around today?

CHRISTIAN PRACTICE

A lot of people say bad things with your name in it, but I never do.

Donald broke the jar NOT me. Now you have it in writing.

I'd like to be a teacher so I can boss people around. I know you're supposed to love thy neighbour, but if Mark keeps taking my other skate, he's going to get it.

On Hallowe'en I am going to wear a Devil's costume. Is that all right with you?

SEX, MARRIAGE AND THE FAMILY

Are boys better than girls? I know you are one, but try to be fair.

The people in the next apartment fight real bad all the time. You should only let very good friends get married.

I went to this wedding, and they kissed right in church. Is that O.K.?

I am adopted. Is that as good as being real?

Did you think up hugging? That is a good thing.

THE CONTEMPORARY SCENE

Church is all right, but you could sure use better music. I hope this does not hurt your feeling. Can you write some new songs?

When you make it rain, how do you know how long to do it?

Do plastic flowers make you mad? I would be if I made the real ones.

Yesterday I had a pizza for luch (*sic*) and spogetie and meat bulls (*sic*) for dinner. What did you have?

Nobody wants to be your buddy when your (*sic*) fat.

I have to know who Shakespeare is before next Friday.

Who draws the lines round the countries?

We read Thomas Edison made light. I thought you did that?

A PERSONAL RELATIONSHIP WITH GOD

I am doing the best I can.

I have pictures of all the leaders except you.

Mrs Coe got a refrigerator. We got the box it came in for a club-house, so that's where I will be if you are looking for me.

I got this new bible and your name is in it. (Love, Teddy)

O.K. I kept my half of the deal. Where's the bike?

We got a lot of religion in our house. So don't worry about us.

DEEPEST THEOLOGY

How did you know you were God?

How do you feel about people who don't believe in you? Somebody else wants to know. (a friend - Neil)

Is mother nature in your family?

What is the use of being good if nobody knows it?

Do you always get the right souls in the right people? You could make a mistake.

I'd like all the bad things to stop.

Instead of letting people die and having to make new ones, why don't you just keep the ones you got now?

ANIMALS

Did you mean for giraffes to look like that, or was it an accident?

Please make it so dogs live as long as people.

How come you didn't invent any new animals lately?

Last week it rained three days. We thought it would be like Noah's Ark, but it wasn't. I'm glad because you could only take two of things, remember, and we have three cats.

If we had fur like the animals we wouldn't have to wear clothes. Did you ever think of that?

CRITICISM

Why isn't Mrs. God's name in the *Bible*? Weren't you married to her when you wrote it?

I know it says turn the other cheek, but what if your sister hit you in the eye?

If we live after we die, why do we have to die then?

My teacher says the North Pole is not really at the top. Did you make any other mistakes?

How come your (*sic*) never on tv?

If you don't want people to say bad words, why did you invent them?

PRAYER

Do you hear us pray to you? It must drive you crazy.

Why don't you leave the sun out at night when we need it most?

Why do I have to pray when you know anyway what I want? But I'll do it anyway if it makes you feel better.

FINAL ASSESSMENT

Your book has a lot of zip in it. I like science fiction stories. You had very good ideas and I would like to know where you found them.

It's very good the way each kid has one mother and one father. Did it take you long to think of that?

If I was God I wouldn't be as good at it.

When I wake up I am glad you left everything right where it was.

If it is in the *Bible* it is true isn't it? Like in the encyclopaedia.

Count me in. (Your friend, Herbie)

ISTHMUS

Contrary to John Donne's thought –
or perhaps complimentarily to it –
every man *is* an island unto himself,
or at least, he feels so -
especially in prison.

St. Paul says we're all in prison –
salutary reminder:
we are our own worst prisons,
even on the Outside.

But prison walls and bars
accentuate the isolation –
really a forced insulation – Elba.
We are made unwillingly into an island:
insulation, without the padding -
(except that worst of cells).
Alcatraz was only closed because of excessive cost:
island home for society's uncontainables.

The island of self is battered most
not by waves of guilt –
the reminders of our erring –
nor by contrition –
gentle, warm, acceptable;
least by penance – soft purification:
but by the unforgiveable wantonness
of unwarranted unmercifulness.

Each day shows signs of man abusing man –
and strangely enough – worse to behold –
a woman abusing men,
in ways as insidious and nasty as blunt.

Bullying is not big boy versus little boy stuff.
It is officers flaying inmates
with the strands of presumed Authority;
it is prisoners torturing the minds of the frail
with some assumed 'seniority' in crime.

It runs in the veins
of unorganised Kafkaesque irrationality;
it is life reduced to spit,
cheap fag-ash, and sneers.

This week, a letter from America –
its stamp torn off –   (*fear of concealed drugs*)
drug search? Philately? Petty theft?

No time for Jeremiads in Time.
There are shining lights
which defeat the darkness within,
within the soul.

One knowing (Christian – sometimes)
human – smile;
one stirring hymn in safe haven prison chapel;
one unasked for compliment about progress;
one reasonable answer to a fair question;
one strong, quiet assertion
that justice will out,
albeit long term;
"God alone is my judge,"
tattoed in ugly blue
on power-builder's shoulder;
one isthmus in the raging waves;
one hand held out by post.
Michaelangelo's hands reach out –
bound to meet:

NO MAN REMAINS AN ISLAND

Workshop Five

A poem written on National Poetry Day, October 6th, 2005 for
Bridging the Gap Competition

In poetry circles, a 'Workshop' is an event
approached with a sense of mystery and trepidation,
earning eventual derision, or ecstatic commendation.
Afterwards, you can always credit yourself with –
"I went to a Workshop at Powys Castle with Gillian Clarke,"
or – "I was at a NATE Conference Workshop with Michael Rosen
in Birmingham (back in the 80s)."
And you think it sounds quite impressive –
or you tell yourself it does.

In **HMP Stafford**, "Workshop" fell on my ears
with a sense of mystery and trepidation,
leading to eventual derision, and much more.
As part of the recuperative, reforming process
that Elizabeth Fry worked so hard for in the nineteenth century,
I approached it with suitable humility,
remorse and gratitude in the twenty first:
here was something to help me see the error of my ways –
humble me, punish me,
and, at the same time, give me a sure foundation
in something useful to Society.

A Fork-lift Truck Driving Certificate
had been muttered about, at "Induction".
My Zimbabwian cell-mate was a brick-layer,
so I fancied getting out and helping a relative
with some artistic landscape-gardening, or extension work.
Rumours told of '*Workshop 10*', with 'challenging recycling work'.
In the '*Sewing Workshop*' there was said to be
an advert for a would-be tailor.
The world was my oyster –
unusual professional training,
with a potential source of income on 'the outside',
in a refreshingly new line of business.
Roll on, *Porridge*! What ho!

But, how to get in on the privilege of workshop selection?
The first thing you have to do is put in an 'Application Form'.
This is tawdrier than it sounds.
It's a sliced-off scrap of paper,
gained legitimately from 'currently out-of-stock' Landing Officers,
or, at the cost of some grams of tobacco,
from an inmate who has hoarded an illicit supply –
a professional form-filler, who knows that sending in an 'Ap'
is like throwing out a bottle with a message in it,
from the coast of Cornwall, and it landing up in Cardiff
for 'actioning' - several weeks later – if at all.

If your Ap is late (?), you miss your place for at least two weeks,
while 'the paperwork is being sorted'.
I was on, 25 days after arriving at Stafford Gaol,
the intervening days designated 'Unemployed',
with 211/2/24 hours 'Banged Up', in preparation.

I approached the metal cage doors of the low-slung factory floor.
My fear was of committing the foolishness of ineptitude,
my academic leanings preferring parsing to technology,
and native cack-handedness being married to extreme insecurity
when it comes to fuses, mouses, spanners - nuts and bolts.

And there they were –
two desultory piles of nuts and bolts,
looking as if they'd been dumped haphazardly
in this off-yellow Sahara of a shop-floor.
Our job was to affix the nut to the bolt
(times thousands per day).
That was all.
They were for roofing experts on 'the outside'.
First thing they would do would be to take the nut off the bolt
- but at least our system guaranteed each bolt had a nut –
(and vice versa).
They were packed up by another table of inmate operands
in packs of 10, at unknown profit to
HMP Stafford Commercial Enterprise Account (via Jewsons).
For us, a 'wage' of £5.30 per 25-hour week,
in the week when HM Government raised the minimum wage
to £5.10 minimum (per hour).

Overhead, Radio One cackled semi-audibly,
like a World War Two desert patrol transmission.
There were no officers wielding batons at us –
just two penguins in white coats – 'Workshop Instructors' –
cruising occasionally between tables,
wanting a quiet time,
dreaming of five o'clock –
the pub, the missus, and Match of the Day –
everything in order - no hassle -
grin – and don't bear it.

In the middle of the hall, the Jamaicans hung out round a table
in a self-ordained ghetto, dying for a game of chequers.
As heat rose, and time didn't fly,
their boredom induced ear-splattering decibels
of incomprehensible badinage,
which wasn't so friendly.
Younger white, macho, 'cool' offenders
started mediaeval warfare,
using plastic spoons to flick lethal nuts at unwary victims.

At a later date – indeed, 28 days later –
after 5 hours' mind-numbing in-activity per day,
5 days per inexorable week,
I graduated to the *Drain-pipe Assembly Line*,
marrying male and female brass ends
to a piece of pipe like a liquorice stick,
hammering in a pin to the respective hole –
or failing to do so.
And then – it was the caravan-trailer warning lights,
to be packed in bubble-paper and plastic, for Halfords,
having started our *Health and Safety in the Workshop Course*,
and signed the *Compact* requiring us to do
'Useful – Productive Work' –
till the chief Workshop Instructor, at end of day, screamed –
"TOOLS!" –
twenty-five purposeless minutes before release to cells:
time for 'rub-down search', for illegal instruments –
crowbars, hatchets, axes, etc – hidden in trouser-legs,
in preparation for the Alcatraz moment.

For the last time, BBC One would hammer out –
for the third repeat of the day –
'*Oasis*' - aptly named, though horribly unavailable
in this sweatshop without sweat,
this living hell, frying the brains –
'*Oasis*' - chanting whiningly, but full of significance,
in a topsy-turvy sort of way, as our anthem:
"*The importance of being idle.*"
Such a scene, in Reading, would have made Oscar wild.

OSCAR WILDE 1854-1900

AN ALPHA-OMEGA OF
'THE DEEPER MEANING OF LIFF'

(WITH ETERNAL GRATITUDE TO DOUGLAS ADAMS AND JOHN LLOYD -1983)

A. **Aalst** (n)   One who changes his name to be nearer the front.

B. **Brumby** (n)   The fake antique plastic seal on pretentious whisky bottle.

C. **Chenies** (pl.n.) The last few sprigs or tassels of last year's Christmas decorations you notice on the ceiling while lying on the sofa on an August afternoon.

D. **Dalfibble**(vb)   To spend large swathes of your life looking for car keys.

E. **Edgbaston** (n) The spare seat-cushion placed against the rear of a London bus to indicate that it has broken down.

F. **Fulking** (pt.pcpl. vb.)   Pretending to be in when the carol-singers come round.

G. **Gallipoli** (adj.) Of the behaviour of a bottom lip trying to spit out mouth-wash after an injection at the dentist. Hence, loose, floppy, useless. 'She went all Gallipoli in his arms.'

H. **Halifax** (n)   The green synthetic Astroturf on which greengrocers greengrocers display their vegetables.

I. **Ible** (adj.) Clever but lazy.

J.   (*entry temporarily unavailable, unless I go back to Stafford*)

K. **Kalami** (n) The ancient Eastern art of being able to fold road-maps properly.

L. **Lambarine** (adj.) Feeling better for having put pyjamas on.

M. **Macroy** (n) An authoritative, confident opinion based on one you read in a newspaper.

N. **Nacton** (n) The 'n' with which cheap advertising copywriters replace the word 'and' (as in 'fish'n chips', ' mix 'n match', 'assault 'n battery'), in the mistaken belief that it is in some way chummy, or endearing.

O. **Ocilla** (n) The cute little circle or heart over an 'i' used by teenage girls when writing their names.

P. **Pant-y-Waccu** (adj.) The final state of mind of a retired colonel before they come to take him away.

Q. **Quabs** (pl.n.) The substances which emerge when you squeeze a black-head.

R. **Radlett** (n) The single hemisphere of dried pea which is invariably found in an otherwise spotlessly clean saucepan.

S. **Spruce Knob** (n) A genital aftershave which is supposed to be catching on in America.

T. **Trunch** (n) Instinctive resentment of people younger than you.

U. **Udine**(adj.) Not susceptible to charm.

V. **Ventnor** (n) One who, having been visited as a child by a mysterious gypsy lady, is gifted with the strange power of being able to operate the air-nozzles above aeroplane seats.

W. **Wedderlairs** (pl.n.) The large patches of sweat on the back of a hot man's T-shirt.

X. (E)**xeter** (n) If you've just mended a fuse, changed a bulb or fixed a blender, the (E)xeter is the small plastic piece left over which means you have to undo everything and start all over again.

Y. **Yalardy** (n) An illness which you know you've got, but which the thermometer refuses to acknowledge.

Z. **Zigong** (n) Screeching skid made by cartoon character prior to turning round and running in the opposite direction.

BOOZE, THE JANUS

The fruits of the vine

As with all of God's gifts,
booze looks two ways –
towards the good, and towards the bad.
The fruits of the vine
(and the workings of the yeast)
accompany us from the cradle to the grave.
A new arrival is toasted in with bubbly –
(nice word - 'toast' – hints of warmth,
fires, and natural camaraderie) –
a traditional 'head-wetting', before the bed-wetting.
Christians in the past presented christening mugs
as an alternative to christening gowns –
a mug of great value, and deep significance.
Cheers! *L'CHAIM!* To Life!

Some good souls enjoy the happy mean:
'booze' is a gloriously non-judgmental word.
The path to Hell is paved with empties, corks and ring-tops.

But the 'happy hour' can be genuinely so,
not just a slither down the inevitable slope.
Rites of passage, birthdays, weddings, anniversaries -
all fêted sparklingly –
congratulations – celebrations –
even inebriations, and hang-overs, and experimentations:
all part of life's full cup.
Life is one long learning bender.

Few have yet decried or condemned outright
pretty harmless customs –
the champagne spray for the Championship Cup;
Flintoff on a double-decker;
the tombola stall at the village Fête
with the Band of Hope looking askance;
the cook injecting the sherry in the trifle,
or the chef flambéing the Christmas pud.
Then, fine wines with the meal,
from Argentina, California, South Africa,
and liqueurs after, or Irish Coffee;
and those nutty-headed home-brewers
with their flagons and plastic siphons:
life constantly bubbling yeast-inspired effervescences.

Let's celebrate the harmless 'booze',
and keep it that way – conviviality –
not descend to binge and baseness,
and blind, bumbling oblivion.
It's so embarrassing – shaming.
It's God's gift – a sin to abuse it.

But pure alcohol's a chemical with an ugly name,
like Methadone, or the sinister Paracetomol, Ethanol.
So when does the worm turn?
It might be in the genes – a family inheritance –
a throw-back to alkie mum, or grand-dad –
(useful, inexcusable excuse, brimful of self-pity).
It's certainly in the nurture, as much as the nature:
alcohol pervades the social ambience.
Good booze habits and bad are equally infectious:
Bon Viveur and *Destroyer*.

Most insidious is the cover-up, the Comforter,
the liquid suppressor of other discomforts,
fighting stress with syrups,
and loneliness with lager;
whipping up anger with whisky,
sousing sorrow in cider.
It's when you're constantly planning the next one,
buying unaffordable supplies –
concealing them -
breathing the inescapable whiff
on innocent, hurt faces.
Letting the god/devil run
and ruin your life
in shameless relapse;
forgetting the present, let alone the past,
and blotting the future:
blotto by choice,
Bacchus despoiled.

Let Janus look forward,
to a clear spring awakening,
not hark back
to our winter of discontent.
It's in our hands –
if we have the bottle.

Seeds, semen, yeast
and the fruits of the vine:
all essentials in God's bounty,
with the in-built capacity for human frailty and sin
to mis-direct, into Hell.

A MUSICAL ALPHA - OMEGA

A. How charming is divine philosophy!   **APOLLO'S LUTE**
   Not harsh and crabbéd, as dull fools suppose,
   But musical as is Apollo's lute.   *Comus 1637 John Milton*

B. Must it be? It must be.   **BEETHOVEN**
   Musses es sein? Es muss sein.
                        Epitaph String Quartet in F major Opus 135

C. You can't stop. Composing's not voluntary,   **COMPOSITION**
   you know. There's no choice, you're not free. You're landed
   with an idea, and you have responsibility to that idea.
                        Harrison Birtwhistle Observer 1996

D. Hell is full of musical amateurs: music is the   **DAMNED**
   brandy of the damned.   *G.B.Shaw Man and Superman 1903*

E. The symphony must be like the world. It must   **EMBRACE**
   embrace everything.
                        Gustav Mahler to Sibelius   Helsinki 1907

F. Fortissimoat last.   **FORTISSIMO**
                        Gustav Mahler on seeing Niagra Falls 1973

G. Gaudeamus igitur,   Let us then rejoice,   **GAUDEAMUS**
   Juvenes dum sumus.   While we are young.
                        Students' song c.1267

H. But all the world understands my language.   **HAYDN**
   on being advised by Mozart in 1790 not to visit England
   because he knew too little of the world, and too few languages.

I. Piping down the valleys wild,   **SONGS OF INNOCENCE**
   Piping songs of pleasant glee,
   On a cloud I saw a child.

                        William Blake 1789

J. Jazz music is to be played sweet,   **JAZZ**
   soft, plenty rhythm.

                        Mister Jelly Roll 1950

K. All people that on earth do dwell,   **KETHE**
   Sing to the Lord with cheerful voice.

                        William Kethe d.1594

L. Give peace a chance. (Song 1969)   **LENNON +McCARTNEY**

M. It is sobering to think that when   **MOZART**
   Mozart was my age he had already been dead.
                        Tom Lehrer 1978

N. There is nothing to it. You only have to hit the **NOTES**
   right notes at the right time, and the instrument plays
   itself. *J.S.Bach, when complimented on his organ-playing.*

O. God-gifted organ-voice of England, **ORGAN**
   Milton, a name to resound for ages.
                            Tennyson-Milton Aleacis 1863

P. Please do not shoot the pianist. He is doing his best.**PIANIST**
         (printed notice in a dancing saloon. Oscar Wilde.
         Impressions of America Leadville 1882-3)

Q. In Quires and Places where they sing, **QUIRES**
   here followeth the anthem.
     Morning Prayer Rubric. The Book of Common Prayer 1662

R. I got rhythm. **RHYTHM**
          'Girl Crazy' 1930 Ira Gershwin 1896-1983

S. O sing unto the Lord a new song: for he **SONG**
   hath done marvellous things. *Psalm 98. 1*

T. The silver, snarling trumpets 'gan to chide. **TRUMPETS**
            Keats The Eve of St. Agnes 1820

U. Take but degree away, untune that string, **UNTUNE**
   And hark what discord follows.
       William Shakespeare Troilus and Cressida 1602

V. The poet ranks far below the painter in the **da VINCI**
   representation of visible things, and far below the musician
   in that of invisible things.
        Irma Richter Notebooks of da Vinci 1952

W. Wagner has lovely moments, but awful quarters **WAGNER**
   of an hour. *Giaachino Rossini 1792-1868*

X. I like Chopin and Bizet, **XCEL**
   and the voice of Gershwin songs
   and old forgotten carols,
   But the music that excels is the sound of oil-wells,
   As they slurp, slurp, slurp into the barrels.
        'An Old-fashioned Girl' Marve Fisher 1954

Y. I hear lake water lapping
   with low sounds by the shore **YEATS**
   I hear it in the deep heart's core.
            Lake Isle of Innisfree 1893

Z. Rock journalism is people who can't write, **ZAPPA**
   interviewing people who can't talk for people who can't read.
          Linda Botts Loose Talk 1980

AN ALPHA-OMEGA OF QUAKERISM

A. Ellan S.Bosanquet (1927) The Inner Light   **AUTHORITY**
does not lead men to do that which is right in their own eyes, but that which is right in God's eyes. As the Light is One, so its teaching is ultimately (though not superficially) harmonious. In actual experience, it is not found that souls looking to the Inner Light as their authority will break away from each other in anarchy.

B. Henry Cadbury (1953) One of the most sobering facts **BIBLE**
is that the Bible is not on the whole a peaceful book – I mean, a book of peace of mind. The Bible is a deposit of a long series of controversies.

C. Susumu Ishitani (1989)   **CONSCIENTIOUS OBJECTION**
The idea of conscientious objection based on the philosophy of non-violence struck me, and was proved to be fair, reasonable and Christian.

D. John Miles (1994) One of the realities of our   **DIVORCE**
meetings these days is that sometimes two people, whom we have come to know as a couple, are unable to sustain their relationship, and decide to separate. It is important to affirm our love for <u>all</u> those who are directly affected, especially if there are children known to the meeting. Above all, the meeting must try to affirm that of God which is in all of us, whatever our feelings about who is to blame.

E. Advice and Queries 2.71 It should be the care of   **ELDERS**
elders to foster the spiritual life of all members, and to give caution and advice to Friends who share in the vocal ministry. They should look out Friends who may be likely to help the ministry and lead them to make their right contribution to the life of their meeting, and to encourage our members to think deeply on the great issues and problems of life and the fundamentals of our faith.

F. Bring into God's light those emotions,   **FORGIVENESS**
attitudes, prejudices in yourself which lie at the root of destructive conflict, acknowledging your need for forgiveness and grace. In what ways are you involved in the work of reconciliation, between individuals, groups and nations?

G. If we take impulses and experiences that are   **GUILT**
potentially wholesome and in a large measure unavoidable, and characterise these as sinful, we create a great volume of unnecessary guilt, and an explosive tension within the personality. A distorted Christianity must bear some of the blame for the sexual disorders of Society.

H. Bill Edgar 1994 "Towards a Quaker   **HOMOSEXUALITY**
View Of Sex" (*n.b.* 1963) It is the nature and quality of a relationship that matters: one must not judge it by its outward appearance, but by its inner worth. Homosexual affection can be as selfless as heterosexual affection, and therefore we cannot see that it is in some way morally worse.

I.   *Yorkshire Quarterly Meeting 1919.* The New   **INCARNATION**
Testament clearly sets out Christ as fully human and as fully divine. It is a pity that we insist on using the term 'humanity' and 'divinity' as though they implied opposition. May we rather not say that Jesus 'shows us the divine life humanly lived, and the human life divinely lived'?

J. Advice and Queries 1.02.04 The Religious Society of   **JESUS**
Friends is rooted in Christianity, and has always found inspiration in the life and teachings of Jesus. How does Jesus speak to you today? Are you following Jesus' example of love in action? Are you learning from his life the reality and cost of obedience to God?

K. Kenneth C. Barnes 1985 It is by **KNOWING AND ACCEPTING**
Knowing our 'imperfections' that we move towards each other, towards wholeness of relationship. It is our oddities, our grittiness, then occasions when we hurt or are hurt that challenge us to a deeper knowledge of each other. Our sins have been said to be 'stepping-stones to God'.

L. *D. June Ellis 1981* The capacity to listen to   **LISTENING**
something is greatly needed, and is an important part of our education, something which has to be worked at constantly. We have a duty to try to help each other to communicate. We must endeavour to meet each other's minds, and we must attempt to achieve not only sympathy, but empathy.

M. William Penn 1693 The humble,   **MULTICULTURALISM**
meek, merciful, just, pious and devout souls are everywhere of one religion; and when death has taken off the mask they will

know one another, though the divers liveries they wear here makes them strangers.

N. Quakers and their Schools 1980 **NON-VIOLENCE**
The Quaker emphasis in education probably lies in non-violence, in participation, and in caring. Not to impose the aims of the school on the pupils, but to lead them to their own acceptance of these aims, to a share (however small) in its running, and a pleasure in its successes. To find that of God in every pupil.

O. Friends believe that their word should be accepted **OATHS** at any time among all persons, and thus uphold the right to stand simply on their word rather than swearing on the Bible or before God.

P. London Yearly Meeting. Our adoption of The World **POLITICS** Council of Church's concern for Justice, Peace and the Integrity of Creation grows from our faith and cannot be separated from it. Ghandi's words: 'Those who say religion has nothing to do with politics do not know what religion means.' The earth's resources must be conserved and shared more equitably.

Q. The key to the development of Quakerism is the **QUAKERISM** understanding of corporate guidance which tests and informs individual leanings. At the heart of this is the meeting for worship where Christ, the Inward Light, is present and is met. George Fox often wrote that Christ has come to teach his people himself. From this teaching comes Quaker faith and practice.

R. John Lampen 1987 Restitution..accepts **RESTITUTION** the reality of what has happened, and the right of the sufferer 'to have something done about it'. It accepts that the perpetrator is in most cases feeling guilty, or at least humiliated to have been detected. But it offers him or her an opportunity to regain the good opinion of the sufferer and the community, and to be seen as a person who can give as well as take away, who can right wrongs as well as cause them.

S. Today Science is rediscovering the creative mystery **SCIENCE** of the universe. The old self-assurance is largely gone. The laws of mechanics no longer explain all things. The intellect of man has become aware of something strange and predictable at the very heart of existence.

T. George Fox. Now I was sent to turn people from **TRUTH** darkness to the light that they might receive Christ Jesus. And I was to direct people to the Spirit that gave forth the Scriptures, by which they might be led into all Truth, and so up to Christ and God.

U. Quaker Faith and Practice. 11.04   Entry into   **UNITY** membership of the Religious Society of Friends is a public acknowledgement of a growing unity with a community of people whose worship and service reflect, however imperfectly, their perception of discipleship and their recognition of the work of the Holy Spirit in the world.

V. If it is right that we show love and   **VEGETARIANISM** compassion for people, surely it is right that we should extend our love and compassion to animals, who can feel and experience pain in much the same way as humans. They may not be able to speak, but we can certainly see fear in their eyes and demeanour.   I feel that being a vegetarian is a natural progression from being a pacifist and a Quaker.

W. George Fox   **WOMEN PRIESTS** *General Epistle 1667*   They that offered in the Jews' temple were to wear the holy garments. So are you to do that are the true Christians, and are called a royal priesthood. What? Are all true Christians priests? Yes. What! Are women priests? Yes, women priests.   The righteousness of the saints is the royal priesthood, which everyone must put on, men and women.

X. Our Society arose from a series of mutual   **THE X-FACTOR** discoveries of men and women who found that they were making the same spiritual pilgrimage. Even at times of great difference of opinion, we have known a sense of living unity, because we have recognised one another as followers of Jesus.

Y. Rejoice in the presence of children and young people **YOUTH** in your   meeting, and recognise the gifts they bring. Are you ready   both   to   learn   from   them,   and   to   accept   your responsibilities towards them?

Z. When all my hopes in all men were gone, **THE FINAL WORD** had nothing outwardly to help me, nor could tell what to do, then, oh then, I heard a voice which said, "There is one, even Christ Jesus, that can speak to thy condition," and when I heard it, my heart leapt for joy.

A PAIR OF POEMS RECORDED FOR THE KOESTLER TRUST PRIZE 2006

TO TOUSSAINT L'OUVERTURE

by

WILLIAM WORDSWORTH AUGUST 1802

(Published in the *Morning Post*)

Francois Dominique Toussaint, surnamed L'Ouverture, was the son of a negro slave. He was imprisoned in Paris in June 1802, because he resisted as Governor of Haiti, Napoleon's edict, re-establishing slavery. He died in imprisonment in April 1803.

Toussaint, the most unhappy Man of men!
Whether the rural Milk-maid by her Cow
Sing in thy hearing, or thou liest now
Alone in some deep dungeon's earless den.
O miserable Chieftain! Where and when
Wilt thou find patience? Yet die not; do thou
Wear rather in thy bonds a cheerful brow:
Though fallen Thyself, never to rise again,
Live, and take comfort. Thou hast left behind
Powers that will work for thee; air, earth and skies;
There's not a breathing of the common wind
That will forget thee; thou hast great allies;
Thy friends are exultations, agonies,
And love, and Man's unconquerable mind.

TO THE (unnamed) ZIMBABWEAN CELL-MATE

by
MICHAEL WILLMOTT

On the day when the British Government suspended the deportation of Zimbabweans back to Mugabe-land - for their 'safety' – thereby separating them from wife and family if they did not allow them to go.

TO M---A

(ON BEING SENT FROM HMP THE DANA TO STOKE CROWN COURT FOR A DEPORTATION DECISION)

M---A, the most unruffled Man of Men,
Whether released, or sent to Detention Centre,
Or, best of worst, to Dana forced to re-enter,
To share with me this high dungeon's earless den,
O miserable chieftain! Where and when
Shall we two meet again? If you concur,
We'll not let time nor space defer
The chance to renew shared toil of Christian.
Quiet liver in this cramped grey cell,
Sharing productive *Guardian* t.t. of t.v.;
Vexed like me by shout, and key, and bell;
Cell's Hygiene Officer – (rather you than me) –
Sensitive to other's pain, whatever it might be,
By faith, and kindness, making Heaven from Hell.

TOM SHARPE 'PORTERHOUSE BLUES'

A Review - by choosing the Top Twenty Sentences
chapter by chapter

1. 'Something to get your teeth into at last,' one of his Cabinet colleagues had said to the new Master, a reference less to the excellence of the College cuisine than to the intractable conservatism of Porterhouse.

2. In the Combination Room the Fellows digested the Feast dyspeptically.

3. Lying awake through the still hours of the night listening to the bells of the College clock and the churches toll the hours, a sound he found mediaeval and unnecessarily premonitory, Sir Godber planned his campaign.

4. All the time Mrs Biggs rattled on with her daily dose of inconsequential information while Zisper dodged about the room like a toreador trying to avoid a talkative bull.

5. Certainly the Honourable Cathcart D'Eath had gone down with a II (ii) in History with his ignorance of Disraeli's influence on the Conservative Party unimpaired in spite of having to all appearances written four pages on the subject.

6. Would Sir Godber have made so many passionate speeches or spoken with such urgency if Lady Mary had been prepared to listen to one word he had said at home?

7. On the Master's left the Bursar fiddled with his pen while on his right the Chaplain, accorded this position by virtue of his deafness, nodded his agreement.

8. Zisper tried to think what he was doing discussing wholesale contraceptive sales with a youngster with a beard in an office in Mill Road.

9. Then he sat down hurriedly in a chair and tried to remember what had happened to him and why he was the possessor of two gross of guaranteed electronically tested three-teat vending machine pack contraceptives.

10. 'When I first came here as Chaplain I used to spend half my time attending inquests. Come to think of it, there was a time when we were known as the slaughterhouse.'

11. Sir Godber: 'All the same, Porterhouse may be the name of the College, but it doesn't mean that the Head Porter is in

charge. On the night of the.. er.. accident, Skullion was distinctly disrespectful.'

12. Sir Cathcart: 'Selwyn! Full of religious maniacs in my time, and Fitzwilliam wasn't a college at all. A sort of hostel for townies.'

13. Whatever the issue, Cornelius Carrington managed to combine moral indignation with entertainment and to extract from the situation just those elements which were most disturbing, without engendering ?

14. The Dean – Carrington. 'You journalist fellows seem to be the carrion crows of contemporary civilization.' He sat back smiling at the happy alliteration of his insult.

15. 'In my view pre-marital intercourse comes into the category of breaking and entering.'

16. Cornelius Carrington's existence depended on his capacity to appear to hold inflexible opinions on nearly every topic under the sun without at the same time offending more than half his audience at once; he spent his life in a state of irresolute commitment.

17. Carrington wheedled out of the Senior Tutor the fact that the annual Feast cost over £2,000, and then went on to ask if the College made any contribution to Oxfam.

18. The Dean preferred his agnosticism straight, and accordingly attended morning service in the College Chapel where the Chaplain could be relied upon to maintain the formalities of religious observance in a tone loud enough to make good the deficiency of his congregation and with an irrelevance to the ethical needs of those few who were present.

19. It had been through the sieve of their indulgent bigotry that young men had squeezed to become judges and lawyers, politicians and soldiers, men of affairs, all of them imbued with a corporate complacency and an intellectual scepticism that dessicated change.

20. (Sir Cathcart's party.) In the interests of several royal guests and unlimited debauchery, masks were worn, if little else.

AN ALPHA-OMEGA OF FOOTBALL

(WITH THANKS TO PETER BALL AND PHIL SHAW)

(with apologies for passé information – book out-of-date)

A. Sam Hamman Wimbledon Chairman 1992 **ACADEMY** "We have to remain the English bulldog SAS Club Club. We have to sustain ourselves by sheer power and the attitude that we will kick ass. We are an academy. We find gems and turn them into finished articles."

B. Eric Cantona: "Everything is beautiful. **BRITISH FOOTBALL** The stadiums are beautiful, the cops on horseback are beautiful. The crowds respect you."

C. Bryan Robson Manchester United Captain **CONSISTENCY** 1990. "If we played like that every week, we wouldn't be so inconsistent."

D. Gary Lineker on Desert Island **DESERT ISLAND DISCS** Discs "I'm a rather boring sort of person."

E. John Lennon: "Anything you say may be **EVERTON** used in Everton against you."

F. John Docherty, Millwall Manager after seven **FAITH** successive defeats, 1989: "There is no crisis here. Just panic."

G .*"Gazza, Daft as a Brush"* – Book title 1989 **GAZZA** "Deft as a brush." *Sunday Correspondent* Headline. "Keep him away from Diana" after Gascoigne described Mrs Thatcher as 'nice and cuddly'.

H. Billy Graham,Evangelist, addressing a rally at **HAMMERS** Upton Park. "I don't know if we can help the Hammers or not, but we're going to pray for them."

I. Ahmed El-Mokadem, Egyptian official, after 0-0 **IRELAND** draw vs. Ireland. "The Irish force an unattractive game on the opposition. No team has managed to escape this contagious crap."

J. Juventus player – "You're done – **JUVENTUS JUSTICE** I'll have you shot, Salvatore Schilloli!" – to Fabio Poli after the Bologna player had slapped his face. 1990

K. Kevin Keagan, after becoming Newcastle Manager **KEEGAN** 1992. "Support means getting behind the team through thick and thin. Newcastle supporters have in the last few years been through thin and thin."

L. Uruguyan-born, Spanish-speaking Manager **LANGUAGE**
Danny Bergara 1991. "Football is a game – the language it don't
matter as long as you run your bollocks off."

M. Jim Duffy - Partick Thistle Captain, **ANDY MURDOCH**
writing uncomplimentarily about his goal-keeper in the club
programme: "Andy Murdoch has an answerphone installed in
his six-yard line and the message says: 'Sorry I'm not in just
now, but if you'd like to leave the ball in the back of the net I'll
get back to you as soon as possible.' "

N. Brian Clough, Nottingham Forest **NELSON MANDELA**
Manager 1990. "I hope you were as delighted as I was last
weekend when Nelson Mandela was freed from a South African
jail. But what I hadn't bargained for was the fact that his release
would cut across the start of our Littlewoods Cup Final."

O. 'Coronation Street' character 1980s: **OLDHAM ATHLETIC**
"Oldham Athletic? That's a contradiction in terms."

P. David Miller *The Times* 1993 **PELE**
"To find a way past him was like searching for the exit from
Hampton Court Maze."

Q. The Dumfries Club are the only **QUEEN OF THE SOUTH**
football team mentioned in the Bible. St. Luke 11.31 – "The
queen of the south shall rise up in the judgement with the men
of this generation and condemn them."

R. Ron Atkinson. West Bromwich after UEAFA Cup **REFEREES**
defeat by Red Star Belgrade, 1979:"I never comment on
referees and I'm not going to break the habit of a lifetime for that
prat."

S. Kevin Keegan, Newcastle Manager, on the prospect **SINGING**
of an all-seater stadium at St. James' Park. " You can't force
people to sit down, even if they have a seat. People want to sing,
and unless you're Val Doonican you can't do that sitting down."

T. Barry Fry,Barnet Manager after 7-4 defeat by **TACKLE**
in First League. "Some of my defenders think a tackle is
something you go fishing with."

U. Ron Atkinson, Aston Villa Manager after 3-0 defeat **USELESS**
at Coventry, 1992. "At least we were consistent: useless in
defence, useless in mid-field and crap up-front."

V. Jack Charlton,Republic of Ireland Manager after **VATICAN**
taking his squad to the Vatican World Cup Finals, 1990: "The
Pope was smaller than I expected, but only in size."

W. Mike Ingham, BBC Radio Sport 1991   **WISE WORDS**
"The governing body of football: television."

X. Gary Lineker addressing the Oxford Union in a   **X-PLAYER** debate on the motion – '*It is better to commentate than to participate.*' "Those who participate provide the poetry. Those who commentate provide the prose. And not very good prose at that. That's why so many players have taken up commentating. It's called missionary work."

Y. "Young man, you couldn't ask me a hard   **YOUNG MAN** question to save your life." Brian Clough, Notts Forest Manager to BskyB reporter, David Livingstone 1992.

No *Z* found.

(**Z**inedin **Z**idane was not available for comment in this 1990's book, selected by ex-Rugby Player, Michael Willmott, HMP Stafford, Christmas 2005)

AN ALPHA-OMEGA OF ANONYMOUS WISE WORDS

(WITH THANKS TO *THE SHORTER OXFORD DICTIONARY OF QUOTATIONS* - EPITAPHS SECTION)

A. Adam / Had 'em.   (*on the antiquity of microbes*)   **ADAM**

B. Bigamy is having one husband too many.   **BIGAMY**
    Monogamy is the same.
                (*epigraph for Erica Jong's 'Fear of Flying' 1973*)

C. 'Rest in peace. The mistake shall not   **CATASTROPHE**
  be repeated.'
            (*inscription on the cenotaph at Hiroshima, Japan*)

D. Death is nature's way of telling you to slow down   **DEATH**
       (*American life insurance proverb, Newsweek 1960*)

E. The rabbit- has a charming face.   **EVASION**
  Its private life is a disgrace.
  I really dare not name to you
  The awful things that rabbits do.   (*1925 The Week-end Book*)

F. "You should make a point of trying   **FOLK-DANCING**
  everything once, excepting incest and folk-dancing."
  (*Arnold Bax, quoting sympathetic Scot. Farewell in Youth 1943*)

G. From ghoulies and ghosties and **GHOULIES & GHOSTIES**
long-leggety beasties, and things that go bump in the night,
Good Lord deliver us.
> (*West Country Litany 1926*)

H. Be happy while y'er leevin, **HAPPINESS**
   For y'er a lang time deid.
> (*Scottish motto for house*)

I. The cloud of unknowing. **IGNORANCE**
> (*title of 14ᵗʰ century mystical work*)

J. Je suis Marxiste – tendance Groucho. **JE**
   I am a Marxist – of the Groucho tendency.
> (*slogan Nanterre 1968*)

K. Kommt der Krieg im Land, Grot's Lugen vie Sand. **der KRIEG**
When war enters a country,/ It produces lies like sand.
> (*epigraph to Arthur Ponsomby 'Falsehood in Wartime' 1928*)

L. An abomination unto the Lord, but a very present help **LIE**
   in trouble.(*Amalgamation of Proverbs 12.22 + Psalm 46.1*)

M. Thought shall be the harder, heart the keener, **MIGHT**
courage the greater, as our might lessens.
> (*The Battle of Malden*)

N. The nature of God is a circle of **NATURE**
which the centre is everywhere and the circumference nowhere.'
Said to have been traced to a lost treatise of Empedocles, quoted
in the *Roman de la Rose*, and by St Bonaventura in *Itinerarius
Mentis in Deum* ch.5 closing line.

O. 'Hereabouts died a very gallant gentleman Captain **OATES**
L.E.G. Oates. In March1912, returning from the Pole, he walked
willingly to his death in a blizzard to try and save his comrades,
beset by hardships.'
(*epitaph on a cairn erected in the Antarctic, 15 November 1912*)

P. Every country has its own **POLITICAL ORGANISATION**
constitution; ours is absolutism moderated by assassination
> (*quote of 'an intelligent Russian 1868'*)

Q. Would you like to sin/With Elinor Glyn **QUESTION**
   On a tigerskin?
   Or would you prefer/ To err with her
   On some other fur?
> (*collected by A. Glyn +Elinor Glyn*)

R. 'If you really want to make a million...   **RELIGION**
   quickest way is to start your own religion.'
      (*Attributed to L. Ron Hubbard Junior, but he dissociated
       himself from it.*)

S. "One Cartwright brought a slave from Russia,   **SLAVERY**
And would scourge him, for which he was questioned: and it
was resolved, that England was too pure an Air for Slaves to
breathe in."
      (*1568-9 Elizabeth 1 – John Rushworth Historical Collections*)

T. So much chewing-gum for the eyes.   **TV**
                  (*small boy's definition of certain tv programmes*)

U. O God, if there be a God, save my soul, if I   **UNCERTAINTY**
   have a soul!
            (*prayer of a common soldier at Blenheim 1704*)

V. It became necessary to destroy the town   **VIETNAM**
   to save it.
                  (*statement by unidentified US Army Major,
                   referring to Ben Tre in Vietnam*)

W. There is so much good in the worst of us,   **WORST**
   And so much bad in the best of us,
   That it hardly behooves any of us
   To talk about the rest of us.
                  (*attributed to amongst others Edward Wallis
                   Hoch 1849-1945 in the Marion Record Kansas,
                   but disclaimed by him.*)

Y. Yankee Doodle came to town   **YANKEE**
   Riding on a pony;
   Stick a feather in his cap,
   And called it Macaroni.

Z. And Zadok the priest took an horn of oil out of the   **ZADOK**
   tabernacle, and anointed Solomon. And they blew the
   trumpet, and all the people said, "God save Solomon."

JACK (PIP) TARR

Winner of the Koestler Spoken Word Prize 2006

Six-foot-five, and an orange pig-tail –
like a character out of Dickens
('charaktairr', he'd call it –
he likes 'charaktairrs')
with a formidable torso
you wouldn't want to come up against
if he was high on *White Lightning,*
and wielding a big stick.
He has *Warfarin* in his long legs –
rat-poison – for the blood clots –
and the other poison in his veins - alcohol –
in quantities that could fuel a motor-bike for miles.

Certainty for inclusion in **HMP The Dana** *Book of Records:*
Longest period out – six months on top of the Wrekin –
shortest 'out' – six days.
Escaping for short periods,
until 'The Three Pensioners' –
the 'magistrate-hags' at Telford
return him to Shrewsbury's Dana.
Last two Christmases there –
the one before in Shelton Hospital.
"Oy will rreeturrn, like the Jedi," he proclaims –
"Oy um an alka-holick."
"We hope we'll never see you again in here,"
they all say, the screws,
knowing he might be back tomorrow morning.

Black Country through and through,
from the language and pronunciation
to the warped, but benign, sense of humour –
e.g. – (topical at Election time):   *(May 2005)*
"When Oy'um sittin' in me tent, on me owe'un,
with me sighdurr" –
(what he calls his liquid food) -
"Oy'um all in a BLAIRR."

On arrival in my cell, he asks :
"How long yow'um bin in fa', then?"
As he goes out, he explains:
"Oy'um just awff fa' me shou'agh,
after me teeya - na wot oy meen?"

In discussion, in high disdain, he explodes:
"Them Mairderrers, them Druggies –
I stick cleair of 'em,
und go un' hide up in me tent in the woo-uds
near 'Apley 'Ouse, or up on the Arcull. (Hapley House; The
Ercall)
I luv it up on top of the Ree-kin (The Wrekin)
out in nature, in the fresh ayer,
with the bairrds, and the animols."

Perhaps short on words, except short ones,
but wide on knowledge, and experience.
Beethoven's *1812 Overture* remembered from his mother.
Knew about Vincent van Gough,
and his yellow flowers, and suicide.
Sided with Ship's Cook on *Mastermind*,
who nearly beat the highly educated writer
with his precise ship's cook knowledge of Muhammed Ali,
and his surprising armoury of odd general facts.
Unbeatable sense of humour,
lapping up the Two Ronnies and Rowan Atkinson,
and telling that one about the man at the bar
betting the company they couldn't respond to this one:
"How high is a Chinaman?"
Answer: "Five foot two?"
"Nah."
"Four foot eleven?"
"Nah."
"Five foot five?"
"Nah. (Flinger on nose.)
HOU HI *IS* A CHINAMAN...HA!"

Spic and span clean,
having been cleaner/orderly in the workshops – for 'burn' money.
Always went to the window out of decency -
to watch the pigeons -
while I crouched on the toilet.
A legend in his time for generosity.
On his last 'canteen' – (weekly supplies from personal money)
he bought the anti-Nazi looney in Cell One, 'Howurrd', some tobacco;
flowers to repay the lady from the DSS,
who'd bought him his best prison-companion – his radio;
sugar and spice, and all things nice
for anyone and everyone at all levels.

Loved by the warders /'screwes', and staff
whom he knew only by their nicknames –
'Mr Fish'- for Mr Haddock – (or sometimes 'Mr Hake')
'Vinegar Tits' – ' the sowerpuss with a forin' nayum,
possibli fram Czeckoslowvakia,
'Fog-'orn' - I hurd 'um call Miss Mack –
Jo – that was it, yesterday, from Liverpooel –
(gave 'im me last 'arf owunce.')

So – off he goes, putting on his 'Going-out Socks',
both pairs of trousers from the cell,
boxer shorts – extra large –
saluting his police escort at the station
with a joyous swig of whisky,
having played his harmonica,
and busked his way to paradise from –
"How far can a man travel before he grows too old?"
to – *"Blowing in the Wind"* –
through the streets of Shrewsbury.

A man of means by no means;
King of the Road –
(or at least the woods);
cell-mate;
soul-mate;
friend for Life.

THE WREKIN, SHROPSHIRE

MY LIFE IN FIFTY WORDS

an entry for the Koestler Prize Short Story Competition 2006

50 WORDS	BIOGRAPHY
EXPECTATION	
CELEBRATION	LODERS VICARAGE,
LACTATION	BRIDPORT, DORSET
INVESTIGATION	26TH APRIL, 1949
IMAGINATION	
*	
SEPARATION	
EDUCATION	
INSPIRATION	SALISBURY CATHEDRAL
INDOCTRINATION	SCHOOL
CONFIRMATION	SEPTEMBER 1958 - APRIL 1963
MILITARISATION	HAILEYBURY & ISC
COLONIALISATION	MAY 1963 – DECEMBER 1967
*	
PEREGRINATION	VSO TURKS & CAICOS IS.
CEREBRATION	1968-1972
EXAMINATION	SELWYN COLLEGE,
	CAMBRIDGE
	*
VOCATION	WATFORD BOYS'
MARITALISATION	GRAMMAR SCHOOL
DOMESTICATION	1972-1977
FAMILIARISATION	12TH August, 1973 Married
URBANISATION	Jo born 23.01.1977
*	
ACCOMMODATION	ADAMS' SCHOOL, WEM
VEGETATION	1977-1982 SHREWSBURY
SALOPIANISATION	Tom born 10.02.1979
RUGBIFICATION	Robin born 17.04.1981
	Shrewsbury Rugby Club
*	
MOTORISATION	HIGHFIELDS SCHOOL,
ORGANISATION	WOLVERHAMPTON
PRESSURISATION	1982-1993
INEBRIATION	Head of English

EXAMINATION
LITIGATION
DISINTEGRATION
SELF-EXTERMINATION
*

VACILLATION   8, BISHOP STREET
EXPERIMENTATION   Shrewsbury
PUBLICATION   BISHOP STREET PRESS
DISSIPATION   1993-2005
CANINIFICATION   Mr. Bean – Labrador-
DIS-RELATION   Pointer
DESPERATION
*

CONFLAGRATION   **April 6th, 2005**
INCARCERATION   HMP THE DANA
*

DESTITUTION   HMP STAFFORD
CONTRITION   **August 2005 -**
RE-CONSTITUTION
ABSTENTION
REHABILITATION
REDEMPTION
EMANCIPATION
EXPECTATION   **March 2006**
*

RESURGENCE   **2006**

Mike Willmott
Oswestry May 2006. Wilfred Owen's Street - after 'Plas Wilmot', Owen's birth-place.

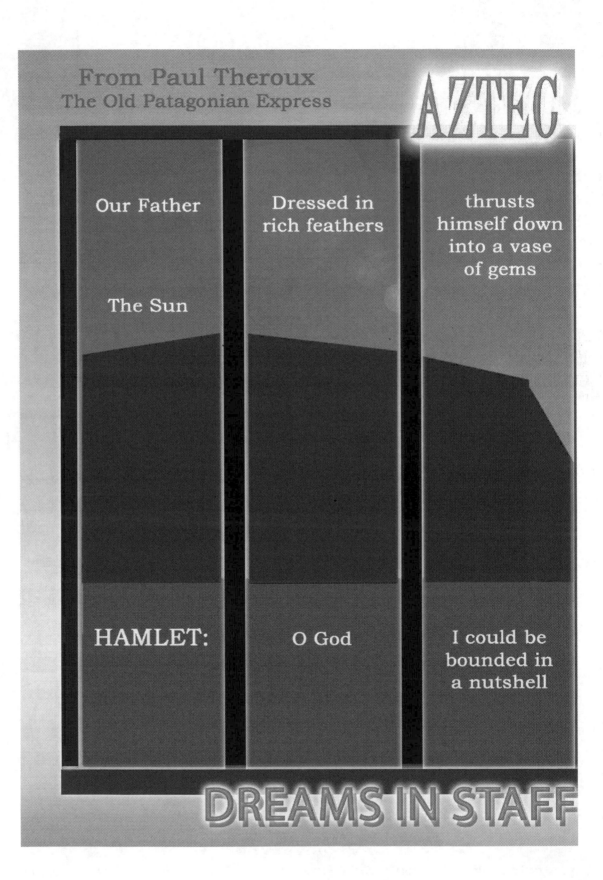

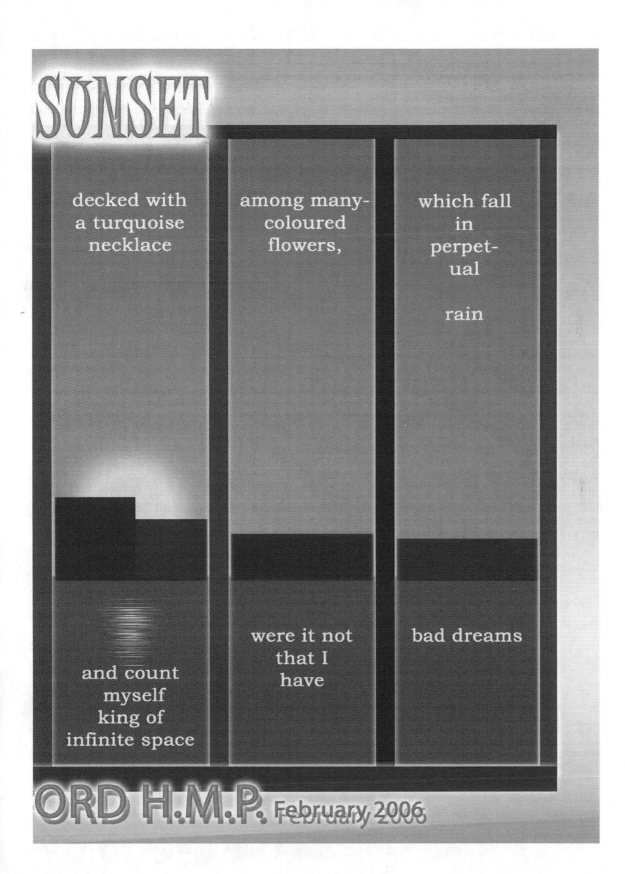

SONSET

decked with
a turquoise
necklace

among many-
coloured
flowers,

which fall
in
perpet-
ual

rain

and count
myself
king of
infinite space

were it not
that I
have

bad dreams

ORD H.M.P. February 2006

63

AN INSIDE LORD'S PRAYER

Our Father, which art in heaven, Our Governor, which art in
high security office,

Hallowed be Thy name; May thy name prove worthy;
Thy kingdom come, May thy most reasonable rules
apply;

On earth, as it is in heaven. And your conscientious
officers carry them out,
Inside, the same as they
should be Outside.

Give us this day our daily bread Give us the best possible
prison food, with more fresh,
less boiled veg, and no steam-
pulped spuds.

Forgive us our trespasses, Forgive us our crimes (when
we've repented),

As we forgive those who trespass And enable us to forgive those
against us. Who may have hurt us.
Lead us not into temptation, Lead us away from temptation,
But deliver us from evil. But spare us from hours of
junk t.v.

For thine is the kingdom, Give us peace of mind, and a
clean heart,
By the power of a benign
prison service,

The power, and the glory, In as short a time as is
possible,

For ever and ever, for full rehabilitation,
Amen. for our men, (and our women).

Aztec Sunset needs a footnote. The graphics represent the pretty accurate dimensions of the view from my cell. There was no horizon, only **HMP Stafford** bricks. Paul Theroux *The Old Patagonian Express* was my last book to read. It coincided with *Songs of Praise* from Patagonia with Aled Jones and hymns from Wales. *Hamlet* has always been a mine of quotation ('For this relief, much thanks.') Prison was a nutshell - and there weren't too many bad dreams. Long live Patagonia!

Printed in the United States
By Bookmasters